Beyond Words: A Collection of Poems

Rohan Jayakrishnan

BookLeaf Publishing

Presentation by *BookLeaf Publishing*

Web: www.bookleafpub.com

E-mail: info@bookleafpub.com

ISBN: 9789358366648

First edition 2023

My Mommy

My mommy is my best friend ever,
My mommy is the cutest girl ever.
My mommy is my Jerry,
The sweetest Jerry ever.
My mommy is my Dora,
The smartest Dora ever.
My mommy is my Cinderella,
The prettiest Cinderella ever.
My mommy is my Minnie,
The most lovely Minnie ever.
My mommy is my best friend ever,
I love her forever.

- RJ (Kindergarten)

My Dad

I want to be like my dad.
I want to get a mustache
And be handsome like my dad.
I want to get a car
And drive it like my dad.
I want to play cricket
And a trophy like my dad.
I want to go to the office
And work on the laptop like my dad.
I want to be the boss always
And be the best like my dad
Because I love my dad.

- RJ (Kindergarten)

My Cutie the Cat

I have a pet cat,
My Cutie the cat.
My grandma takes care of
My Cutie the cat.
My cat is grey in color,
My Cutie the cat.
My cat cries, "Meow, Meow, Meow"
My Cutie the cat.
One day, my grandma gave fish to
My Cutie the cat.
My Cutie the cat-
Didn't like the fish.
So my Cutie the cat spit the fish.
So my Grandma became sad,
And fried the fish.
My Cutie the cat
Ate the fish and said "Yummy"
My Grandma was happy!

- RJ (Kindergarten)

The Spring

Spring, Spring, Spring
It's time for spring.
We can have fun in the spring,
We can smell flowers in the spring,
The flowers bloom in the spring,
Baby leaves grow in the spring,
The butterflies and bees come in the spring,
The birds chirp in the spring,
The squirrels look for acorns in the spring,
The goose swims in the spring,
It rains in the spring,
We can see the rainbows in the spring,
I like to play in the spring,
I enjoy the spring,
Spring, Spring, Spring!

- RJ (Grade 1)

The snow

Snow, Snow, Snow
Snow, so white,
Light and bright!
It is fun to play-
With the snowballs
And to make a snowman with snow.
It is fun to play-
Like the snow angels
And to sled in the snow.
Yippee! Yippee!
Hurray!
Snow is fun all day,
Snow is awesome!

- RJ (Grade 1)

Save the Earth

Save Save Save
Save the earth.
Plant more trees,
Save the seas.
Clean the air,
To protect the ozone layer.
Cut down the plastic bags and bottles,
And use reusable ones.
Throw the trash
In the garbage bins.
Everyone needs to save the earth,
The earth who gave us birth.
Our Mother Earth
Save Save Save!

- RJ (Grade 1)

The spooky spooky halloween

When it's October
And the leaves fall down,
It is time for halloween,
The spooky spooky halloween.
We wear our costumes
Of different kinds,
We trick-or-treat
Our friends we meet.
The fluttering bats, owls,
Jack-o-lantern, spooky trees,
Witch on a broom stick,
Vampires, scary skeletons,
With the spiders all around
On a very dark night
With only the spooky moon light
Are scary part of halloween.
Candies, candies and candies
Are the sweetest part of halloween.
It is fun to be on a Halloween,
The spooky spooky Halloween!

- RJ (Grade 1)

The boy named Billy

There once was a boy named Billy.
He fell off his bike 'cuz he was silly.
Poor guy was hospitalized in CHOP,
Surely couldn't hop.
So he returned home when it became chilly.

-RJ (Grade 5)

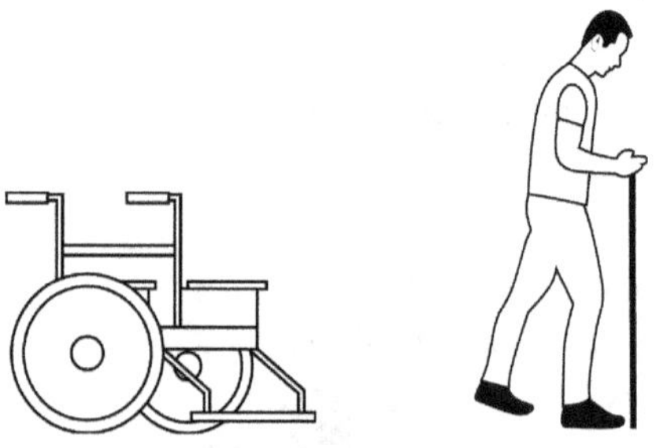

Memory

In third grade
I still remember the day
October 31.
I had came back from the hospital
It felt like a year, stuck in a deep creepy cave.
I was a pirate
In a wheel chair.
My amazing mom pushing me,
And getting all the candy
For me, me, me.
I was the sun,
And my parents were orbiting.

That night someone asked me
"Is the wheelchair part of the costume?"
Before I could
My mom said "Yes" like she meant it.
I didn't understand why?
That day I was so thankful,
Thankful that I had a wonderful mom
an angel just for me!

- RJ (Grade 5)

Analysis on the clarinet

It's about
The mouthpiece,
The ligature,
The reed,
The barrel,
The top set of keys,
The bottom set of keys,
The bell,
And your effort.
Reed vibrates for sound,
Keep tongue high,
And blow good air, very good air
And beautiful sounds like natures music
Will come right out.
Press down the keys
Different notes come out.

Concerts, band
Playing around.
Listening to other sounds,
Bringing the crowd,
Practice, effort,
Determination, commitment,
Important roles, and
important goals.
Important, Important, Important

As small as and aboe,
But projects sound
As loud as a trumpet,
The clarinet

- RJ (Grade 6)

This year

Things are going to be different this year
Because I'm going to study harder in math
Remembering that proportions are different than
ratios.

Things are going to be different this year
Because I'm going to play harder in P.E,
Impressing my friends and family, too
With my hard work and talent.

Things are going to be different this year
Because I won't be in the same class for the
whole day
Or take the same bus, with no space to sit
I won't even have to be with the mean bullies.

Things are going to be different this year
Because I'm going to learn medical science
So I can become a doctor and show off my
surgical skills
And my family will be proud and amazed
And maybe someday, my riskful work will
Be heard all around the world.

- RJ (Grade 6)

Life doesn't frighten me at all

Darkness fills up the room
Bugs are crawling in my shoes,
Life doesn't frighten me at all.
My grades go down
I have a big frown,
Life doesn't frighten me at all.

Playing basketball
With my friends and all,
Laughter on my face
There is no disgrace,
Going to school
Learning new things, so cool,
Having a fun family
Doing things so joyfully,
Life doesn't frighten me at all.

- RJ (Grade 6)

Waterpark

In the car
Along the mountains
Out of the car
After breakfast
Into the changing rooms
Towards the pool
Under the water
Out of the pool
Towards the rides
Onto the coaster
Down the thrill
Through the loop
Into the hot tub
Into clean cloths
At the end of the day
On my 11th birthday
Having fun at Great Wolf Lodge!

- RJ (Grade 6)

Summer

Summer is the best season.

Summer is green grass and the beauty
Of Aurora Borealis.

Summer smells like freshly cut grass
Which is greener on the other side of the fence.

Summer tastes like ice cream
On a hot sunny day.

Summer sounds like kids
Having fun in the neighborhood.

Summer feels like heavenly powers
Carrying you to your dreams.

People playing, traveling, enjoying.

Summer is ultra-epic-awesome-
Enjoyable-super-duper-amazing.

Summer is the Michael Jordan
Of all seasons

Summer is just the best and
There's nothing that can change it.

- RJ (Grade 7)

Oh widow!

Oh Widow! Poor Widow!
How sad you must be.
You lost him in a World War,
And he's not by thee.

Oh Widow! Poor Widow!
How impossible it must have been
To take care of a child,
With help nowhere to be seen.

Oh Widow! Brave Widow!
How courageous you must be
To carry on a child,
After a tragic history.

Oh Widow! Proud Widow!
How proud you must be
The child whom you've treasured
Is all grown up and successful; isn't he?

- RJ (Grade 7)

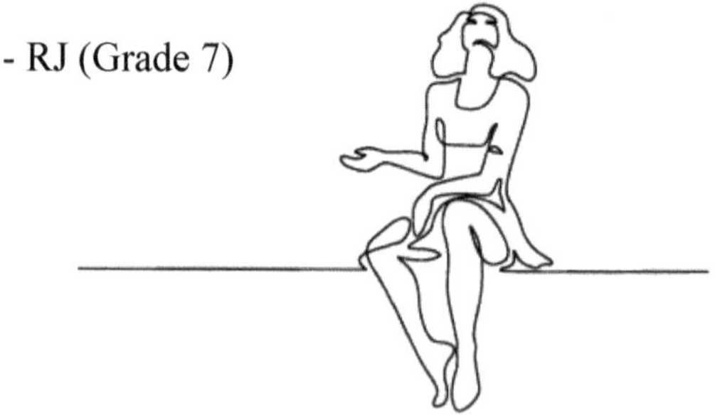

The end

There I was,
On a couch just chillin'.
Drinking soda, SIP
Trying not to be spillin'.

Amber Alerts, News Flashes,
What was happening
The screams outside, EEK
My heart dampening

I look outside and chaos breaks
Chaos, like after Thanos snapped his fingers
As the terrible townspeople taunted each other
My eyes slowly feel the pain of bee stingers

There were cracks in Mother Earth
The buildings falling apart
And darkness creeping upon us
Our lives were going to depart

I cried out for my family
Tears fill the room
I knew it was the end
The world meeting its doom.

- RJ (Grade 8)

I'm from

I'm from the depths of my welcoming room,
From bright artwork and RC cars that go vroom!
I'm from the colorful, spacious area,
The culturally equipped place I call, "Home!"
I'm from the roots of coconut trees, it flows
through my veins,
From the bushes of azalea who shine with grace,
Whose color is exquisite, light pink, and
glittering.
I'm from celebrating with a get-together and big
feast for Onam,
From Nanda and Jayakrishnan
I'm from speaking our language at home,
And humming tunes when we're bored
And from watching shows as a family.
I'm from reaching for the stars and never letting
anything stop me
And the musical notes of "Welcome to My
House".
I'm traveling, from the depths of the ocean to
The vivacious greenery of Kerala
Where the relaxing rain dampens against the
grass.
The sweet, savory banana fritters
And buttery dosa with yummy sambar.

A copper tub, decorated and handled down from
generations,
People whom I love and hold dearly to my heart.
My mom, dad, and grandparents, whom I
cherish
I am from moments and memories which-
I wouldn't trade it for the world!

- RJ (Grade 8)

I am unique

I am unique
My love for drawing and music,
The colors and musical notes,
Flowing through my mind.

I am unique
Chinese food is just the best,
The sweet, savory flavors ,
Overwhelming my tastebuds.

I am unique
Nature is my getaway,
The fresh air flowing,
Cooling me with its gentle push.

I am unique
Traveling can never be tiring,
The beautiful sights,
To be cherished with friends and family.

I am unique
I can't live without family,
Cherishing every moment,
Spending every moment together.

Uniqueness
The wonder of being diverse
Like the rainforest filled with an abundance of
species

- RJ (Grade 8)

Dear May

Without you,

          I am birthday-less,

My feelings,

          My birth,

Numb,

          Gone,

Like the flowers,

          In the depths of a

desert,
I try to bloom,

          In the dryness,

Stay with me

          Let's enjoy,

Let's open presents

          Have fun,

Like two siblings,

          Spend all the time

we have,
Together.

P.S. You are my favorite month of the year

- RJ (Grade 8)

Fall

Fall, just around the corner.
The leaves flutter through the brisk breeze.
Like English words through the mind of a
foreigner,
Like droplets of a sharp sneeze.

Red, orange, brown, yellow,
The vibrance becomes tyrannic
Tyrannizes over the green leaves.
As the warmth becomes panic.

The heat turns cold,
Humid turns to the breeze.
"So darn cold" said the old,
And so the sweat said, "freeze"

No matter the weather,
No matter the breeze,
Fall will be fall,
And I can say that with ease.

- RJ (Grade 9)

Paradise

Shores brighten up in this sky,
We are reaching an unseen world,
The stories go endless like the depth of the sea.

No one cries here.
No one will stop your smiles
No bitterness from any past woes.

A new lease of life it is, and this is your paradise,
The paradise of joy.

Let them sing as long as they can.
Let them dance until they tire.
Let them fill their body with an utter sense of joy.
Partying, Dancing, Singing, Playing

And that's your paradise
The paradise of joy.

- RJ (Grade 9)